"If you believe that people h.... ...ntioning,
it's easy to believe they have ?. ...y worth defending."

\- William Loren Katz

Abandoned History Series

This book is part of the Abandoned History Series published by the Museum of disABILITY History, People Inc., and People Ink Press.

Due to a general reluctance to discuss the way those in need were treated in the past, records and memories related to the care and treatment of the poor, sick, and disabled are fading into the past – into the world of abandoned history.

The Museum of disABILITY History is committed to preserving the important historical record of these almost-forgotten lives and the institutions and services that evolved over centuries to provide a more humane existence for those in need of care.

This book is a part of that effort.

Design by Rachel Gottorff, People Inc.

Publisher: Museum of disABILITY History

ISBN 13: 978-0-9845983-8-0

Library of Congress Control Number: 2012951443

People Ink Press
in association with the
Museum of disABILITY History
3826 Main Street
Buffalo, New York 14226

Cover image: Shown is a AC All-Weather tricycle pictured in 1951. In Great Britain, the red "L" on a motorbike means "learner" and serves as a provisional license that limits the size and operation of motorbikes on roadways until motorists have obtained substantial experience and additional training.

PEOPLE INK PRESS

An Introduction to the British Invalid Carriage
1850 – 1978

Stuart Cyphus

1955 Invacar Mk 8A pictured when new. It was vehicles such as these that helped a generation of disabled persons toward a new independence.

The Invalid Carriage Register (ICR) was founded in 1995. The ICR is the only organization in the United Kingdom covering the historical aspects of transport for the disabled in all its forms, from the bath chair of the 1800s to the modern pavement scooter of today, with particular emphasis on the powered invalid three-wheelers as featured in this publication.

Further details can be obtained from Stuart Cyphus, 6 Mirfield Road, Witney, Oxfordshire, OX28 5BA.
Email: invacar@yahoo.co.uk

1

The Development of an Industry

The history of specialized wheel transport for disabled persons in the UK spans over 160 years, having its origin in the humble Victorian wickerwork bath chair, a vehicle that first began to appear in the 1840s and did not fully fade away until the 1950s.

For the first one hundred years, progress was slow, but on July 6, 1948, came the foundation of the Ministry of Health's National Health Service (NHS) with its famous brief of providing a "comprehensive and free health service for every man, woman, and child in the country, from the cradle to the grave." Within the National Health Service also came the attendant establishment of the Invalid Vehicle Service, in which invalid three-wheelers in both powered and hand-propelled forms would be issued free of charge by the NHS to any disabled person meeting the necessary criteria.

Within the Invalid Vehicle Service, the invalid three-wheeler developed rapidly during the 1950s, moving away from its bath chair origins toward something approaching a modern saloon car via a torturous route of weather protection and bodywork. In 1957 the transformation was completed when the Ministry of Health introduced the "standard specification" of running gear fitted to internal combustion invalid vehicles, stating their preference for the 197cc Villiers Mk 9E two-stroke engine fitted with SIBA Dynastart.

What's in a Name: Carriage or Tricycle?

When the first powered invalid three-wheelers began appearing after World War I, nobody knew precisely what to call these machines. The terms, "motor bath chair" and "motor invalid chair" were both in use but were far from satisfactory. The problem was finally solved by the Ministry of Transport's Road Traffic Act of 1930, which finally defined such vehicles as "...Invalid Carriages, that is, mechanically propelled vehicles, the weight of which unladen does not exceed five hundredweight (560 pounds) and are specifically designed and constructed and not merely adapted for the use of persons suffering from some physical defect or disability and which are used solely by such persons..."

On January 1, 1960, Section 12 of the Vehicle Excise Act created, alongside the long-established invalid carriage, a new class of invalid three-wheeler in the form of the invalid tricycle. The fundamental differences between the two types were that an invalid carriage weighed less than 560 pounds and was restricted to a 20 mph top speed, while an invalid tricycle weighed between 560-672 pounds and was completely unrestricted in speed other than by the limits of engine power.

Thus, a 1947 Argson De Luxe is an invalid carriage, whereas a 1977 Model 70 is an invalid tricycle. Also, the regulations stated that a tricycle could legally be driven upon a motorway but a carriage could not. Contrary to popular opinion, these regulations are still in force today.

The End of the Road?

On July 23, 1976, after many years of applied pressure from militant campaigners, the Department of Health and Social Security (DHSS) announced the closure of the Invalid Vehicle Service to new applicants in view of "increasingly hostile reactions" and "technical difficulties." At that time, the DHSS had 21,500 invalid three-wheelers in its fleet and intended that all would be withdrawn from service by 1981. As it happened, the very last "Ministry" Model 70 was not collected in until October 14, 2004.

And there the 160 year history of the invalid three-wheeler would have ended, however, with today's presence of the electric mobility scooter, very similar in principle to the earliest powered machines produced at the time of World War I, has not the story come full-circle?

HAND PROPELLED TRICYCLES

Almost every manufacturer charted within this booklet produced a hand-propelled invalid tricycle of one sort or another in addition to their motor models. The first concern to introduce a hand-propelled tricycle was Carter (J&A) Ltd. in 1879, while the last to discontinue such a device was R.A. Harding (Bath) Ltd. in 1973.

In general, there were two distinct types of hand-propelled tricycles, the first being a rear-steer machine in which the single wheel

was at the rear and steered by movements of the seat's backrest. It featured rotary propulsion that was affected by bicycle-type pedals and chained to one or both front wheels.

Shown is a 1968 Harding Netley.

CARTER
(J&A) LTD.

The long-established London-based company of Carter (J&A) Ltd. introduced the industry's first successful electric invalid carriage in the Carter Model A in 1915. Over the years, the Carter electric carriage was developed until about 1936, when the final and most commonly seen variants of the range were introduced as Models E, F, and G.

In terms of general appearance, the 24-volt Model E and 36-volt Model F were both traditional open tricycles. At the top of the range, however, was the 36-volt Model G, which followed the same basic layout as the Model F but had enclosed bodywork extending forward from the seat to protect the driver's legs and a door on the nearside to provide entry.

Production of the Carter range of electric three-wheelers is believed to have ended in 1955.

Shown is a 1941 Carter Model F.

G.H. Dingwall & Sons (Engineers) Ltd. was founded in Dalston, London in 1870 for the manufacture of invalid furniture. Their first hand-propelled tricycle was announced in 1892 and their first motorized tricycle appeared at the end of 1922. By the end of the 1930s, the company introduced their mainstay De Luxe Motor Tricycle, powered by a 147cc Villiers Mk VIIIC engine and priced at £175 ($222 U.S.) in 1946.

In June 1953 the Dingwall company announced an addition to

their range of hand and motor-propelled tricycles in the form of a motor-assisted tricycle that managed to set a wheel firmly in both camps but with a 32cc Berini cyclemotor driving directly on the front tire.

Powered Dingwall production ended around 1953. In 1960 the company was acquired by its chief designer, Mr. M.T.B. Harty and was renamed Harty Dingwall Ltd. to continue production of hand-propelled machines.

Shown is a 1946 Dingwall De Luxe.

Founded in 1921, the R.A. Harding company of Lower Bristol Road, Bath, produced hand-propelled tricycles before introducing their first motor models in 1926. In pre-war years, the powered Harding range included the 122cc Villiers-powered De Luxe Models A and B, the 200cc or 300cc J.A.P.-powered Pultney and 24-volt or 36-volt electric machines.

In 1945 the company was renamed R.A. Harding (Bath) Ltd. and the Pultney was discontinued. In December 1948 the "New"

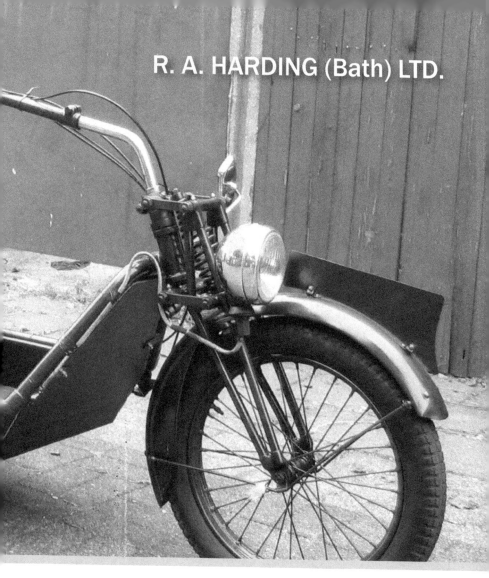

Harding De Luxe Models A and B were announced with larger rear wheels, a new petrol tank and a fan-cooled Villiers 147cc unit in place of the 122cc engine.

In 1956 the company introduced the unsuccessful full-bodied Consort Model, of which only twelve examples were made. In 1966 the entire range of powered Harding vehicles was discontinued, but hand-propelled machines continued to be offered until 1973.

Shown is a 1954 De Luxe Model A.

THE TRILOX

The Trilox company of Trowbridge, Wiltshire, was founded in the 1920s by Albert Jones and produced a large range of hand-propelled tricycles before entering the field of motorized vehicles in the 1930s with the Trilox Rollsette.

Over the years, both Villiers petrol and 36-volt electric versions of the Rollsette were produced. A distinct feature of the Rollsette was always the plywood "box" which offered some protection for the driver's legs. After the Second World War, a new addition to

the Trilox range was seen in the form of the Tricar, with improved bodywork and fitted hood and windscreen. Again, both petrol and electric versions were offered.

Production slowly dwindled away during the mid-1950s. Plans were in hand to introduce an all-new electric tricycle in 1959 but the Trilox company was never heard of again after that date.

Shown is a 1948 petrol Trilox Rollsette.

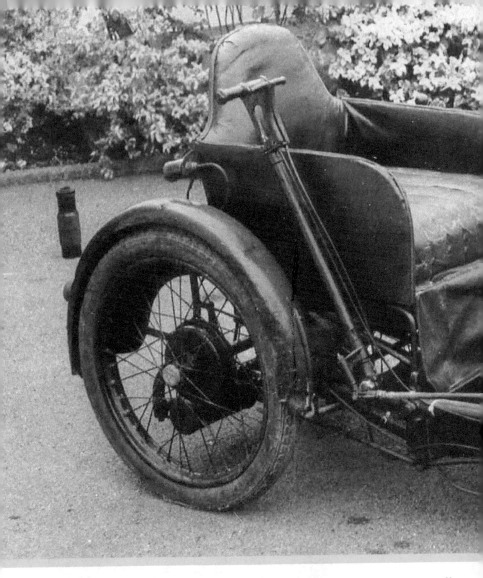

Founded in 1919, the Argson Engineering Company was originally based at Twickenham where it produced hand-propelled tricycles. In 1922 the Argson concern introduced the industry's first purpose-built motor tricycle after fitting an engine of their own manufacture to one of these machines.

In 1926 the Argson Engineering Company was renamed the Stanley Engineering Company following a move to Egham. The original Argson Motor Tricycle was replaced at this time by the

Argson De Luxe and Standard Models, both fitted with 147cc Villiers engines. The Runnymede introduced in 1934 had the same engine but detail differences in the chassis.

In 1946 came the Argson Victory, replacing the Runnymede. Always following the traditional "open" style, the last petrol Argsons were produced in 1953. Stanley engineering was taken over in early 1954 by C.B. Harper Ltd., who introduced their own range of invalid three-wheelers.

Shown is a 1937 Argson De Luxe.

THE
ARGSON
ELECTRIC

Introduced in 1923, the 36-volt Argson Electric was the most common variant of all Argson invalid carriages. Although the vehicle itself came from the Stanley Engineering Company, the patented combined steering and motor speed control unit in which the steering bar was twisted clockwise to select forward-speed ranges or counterclockwise to select reverse-speed ranges was developed independently by Leonard Murphy.

In 1946 the Ministry of Health ordered their first batch of Argson Electrics for supply to war pensioners, the Argson being the staple "Ministry" electric machine until 1954.

In March 1951 the original Argson Electric gave way to the new Argson Electric De Luxe, which had a new control box fitted at the left-hand side of the redesigned seat. Following the takeover of Stanley Engineering by C.B. Harper Ltd. early in 1954, the Argson Electric was finally discontinued in December of that year. Roughly 8,000 were produced.

Shown is a 1954 Argson Electric De Luxe.

Introduced in 1929, the 36-volt Nelco Solocar had quite a complicated early history. Originally known as the Auto-Electric Carriage, it was another design from the pen of Leonard Murphy and the result of a disagreement between him and the Argson company regarding the development of his patented control box system, as seen in the Argson Electric.

During 1947 the Auto-Electric Carriage underwent a major restyling of its rear bodywork and a change of name that completed

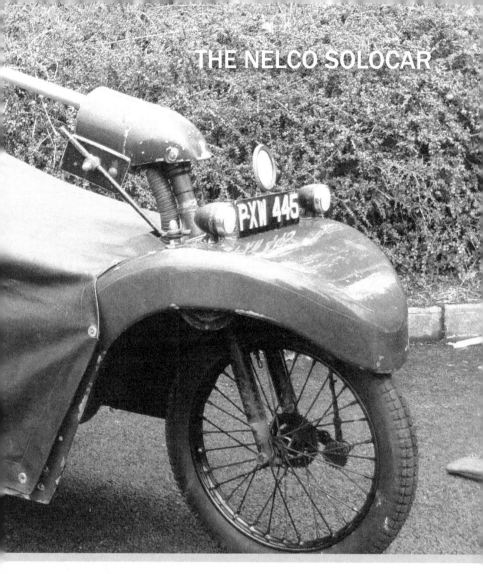

its transformation into the well-known Nelco Solocar. In December 1952 production rights were sold to the long-established Reselco Invalid Carriages company of Hammersmith, London.

Regardless of some beliefs, the Solocar was not rebadged as the Reselco Solocar following the Reselco takeover. It continued as the Nelco Solocar until the end of production in March 1967 after 38 years and some 3,000 examples produced.

Shown is a 1955 Nelco Solocar.

THE LARMAR CAR

Announced in 1946, the four-wheeled Larmar Car was a complete departure from current disabled-vehicle designs in that it resembled an ordinary car. Powered by a rear-mounted 249cc BSA four-stroke engine, the Larmar was intended by its designers to fit through a standard domestic house doorway, thus enabling owners to park the car in the hallway of the house if no outside storage space was available. As such, the Larmar was only 2 feet and 4 inches wide.

The Larmar Car had an enthusiastic following amongst more sensitive disabled persons due to its "ordinary car" appearance, but this very desirability attracted the attentions of H.M. Customs and Excise, which levied the full amount of purchase tax upon it, destroying its appeal almost overnight.

In 1949 the Larmar Model B was introduced. It was eight inches wider than the original to accommodate a folding wheelchair alongside the driver. Production ended in 1951.

Shown is a 1946 Larmar Car.

INVACAR LTD. 1946-1952

When the first machines of Bert Greeves and Derry Preston-Cobb's Invacar Ltd. took to the roads in March 1946, they were hailed as the industry's greatest leap forward technologically since the first powered vehicles of the 1920s due to each vehicle being tailored to suit the individual, something the industry had not done to any great extent before.

Powered initially by 122cc Villiers Mk 9D engines, with the 197cc Mk 6E offered from 1948 mounted on the right-hand side of

the chassis directly ahead of the rear wheel, the Invacar immediately wrested the industry's "number one" spot from Argson and remained there for the next thirty years.

Over the years, many details, improvements, and refinements were made to the basic vehicle, including rudimentary weather protection. Its high regard within the industry was further bolstered by Invacar Ltd. gaining substantial Ministry of Health supply contracts in 1949.

Shown is a March 1947 second-produced Invacar Model 12.

Introduced in 1950, the A.C. All Weather produced by A.C. Cars Ltd. of Thames Ditton was the result of a protracted government debate on the adequacy of weather protection (which was mostly non-existent) on invalid three-wheelers currently being supplied to the country's war pensioners.

Powered by a 249cc BSA C10 engine mounted under the seat, the tubular backbone chassis supported a fully enclosed steel and aluminum bodyshell with a large double-fold door on the nearside

to aid entry and exit. At the rear, a large trunk enabled a folding wheelchair to be carried.

The All Weather Mk 2 was introduced in 1951 but production halted in August 1952 following a series of flash fires and ever-growing production costs. For many years the A.C. All Weather was feared extinct, with the last reported sighting in Norfolk during 1974. However, in May 2004 a surviving Mk 1 example was finally located in Essex.

Shown is an AC All-Weather tricycle pictured in 1951.

Announced in September 1950, the Fitt Continental was the industry's last new design of "open" tricycle. It owed much of its layout to the contemporary Invacar product, with its 197cc Villiers Mk 6E engine mounted on the side of the chassis in front of the right-hand rear wheel. As with the Invacar, right-hand tiller steering with tiller braking was also fitted.

Although ungainly in appearance, with a box-section chassis, very large rear wheels, and an exceptionally small front wheel, the

Continental was one of the first tricycles to be fitted with independent rear suspension, effected by rubber blocks.

Built primarily for the Ministry of Health, which ordered 500 models, most were recalled by the Ministry after production ended in 1953 to be fitted with weather protection. At the time of this writing, there are no known examples of the Fitt Continental in existence. All 500 are believed to have been scrapped by the end of the 1960s.

Shown is a 1950 publicity picture for the Fitt Continental.

THE
INVACAR
MK 8 & 8A

In February 1952, Invacar Ltd. replaced their original 1946 range of vehicles with a single weather-protected model in the form of the Invacar Mk8. Built upon the same chassis, all examples were powered by the 197cc Villiers Mk 8E engine and had a fixed hood and windscreen with leather cloth 'panels' stretched over a welded tubular frame bolted to the chassis to form the complete body shape and roof.

In February 1955, the Invacar Mk 8 gave way to the Mk 8A, which was fitted with rubber-in-torsion rear suspension and had a larger and wider one-piece hood that now covered the rear petrol tank completely and also incorporated a much larger rear window.

In July 1955, Invacar Ltd. produced a small batch of Mk 8B machines fitted with twin-cylinder 242cc British Anzani engines in place of the 197cc Villiers unit. Production of the standard Invacar Mk 8A continued until late 1956.

Shown is a 1952 Invacar Mk 8.

THE
VERNON
INVALID
CAR

Vernon Industries Ltd. entered the invalid carriage market in 1950 by building a version of the original Invacar under license; however, following the introduction of the new Invacar Mk 8 in 1952, this license was canceled, prompting the Vernon concern to develop their own machine in direct competition.

Unveiled in February 1955, the Vernon Invalid Car (often incorrectly contracted to Vi-Car) was very similar in principle to the Invacar Mk 8, with its side-mounted Villiers Mk 8E engine, but the Vernon design incorporated a wooden-framed aluminum-clad body. In late 1955, the Vernon Invalid Car Mk 2 was introduced, fitted with a slightly modified all-metal body.

Mostly produced to Ministry order, the Vernon Invalid Car Mk 3 appeared in April 1957, fitted with the Villiers Mk 9E engine and Dynastart to bring it into line with the new Ministry Standard Specification. Production ended in March 1958, with none of the 1,500 produced known to exist at the time of writing.

Shown is a Vernon Invalid Car Mk 1 publicity picture of 1955.

THE
HARPER
MARK
1 & 4

Following the takeover of the Stanley Engineering Company by C.B. Harper Ltd., the entire range of Argson tricycles was withdrawn from production to be replaced by a new breed of 'Harper' invalid carriages, introduced in July 1954.

With current trends in the general invalid carriage industry leaning ever further towards saloon bodywork, the new Harper Mk 1 had a full bodyshell molded from fiberglass. Two versions of the basic vehicle were offered: a petrol model powered by a rear-mounted 197cc Villiers Mk 8E/R engine, and a 36-volt electric model. Both versions shared the same body and chassis.

In July 1956, the Harper Mk 1 was replaced by the improved Mk 4, again offered in both petrol and electric forms, in which the shared bodyshell had been redesigned to incorporate a wider windscreen and depressed moldings on the body sides for greater strength and reduced resonance.

Only one example of a Harper Mk 1 is known to exist today.

Shown is a 1954 publicity picture of a Harper Mk 1.

THE
HARPER
MK 6

On the introduction of the Ministry of Health Standard Specifications, the Stanley Engineering Company replaced their Harper Mk 4 in April 1957 with the very much larger Harper Mk 6. As with its predecessor, the Mk 6 was offered in both petrol and 36-volt electric forms, both versions again sharing the same chassis and fiberglass body.

In 1959, Stanley Engineering built six 'Harpermatic' versions of the Harper Mk 6, in which the conventional, manual gearbox was replaced by a constantly variable transmission, marking the first use of an automatic gearbox in a petrol invalid three-wheeler. Much was hoped for at the time, but the future development of automatic transmissions in such vehicles stalled until the arrival of A.C. Cars Ltd. Model 70 in 1971.

In 1960, the Harper Mk 6 was renamed the Stanley Mk 7, and gained a higher roof, glass side windows and a Villiers Mk 11E power unit. Production ended in 1965.

Shown is a 1960 publicity picture of a Stanley Mk 7.

THE
INVACAR
Mk 10

Replacing the old canvas-bodied Invacar Mk 8A, the 1957 Invacar Mk 10 was a direct result of the Ministry of Health's 1957 mechanical Standard Specification notice. Invacar Ltd. abandoned side-mounted engines in favor of a rear-mounted Villiers Mk 9E power unit.

On its introduction, the Invacar Mk 10 amazed the industry by having a pressed-steel bodyshell. Even more remarkable, despite the heavyweight body, the Mk 10 weighed only 550 lb. unladen, meaning that it still conformed to the official 560 lb./5 cwt. overall weight limit for an invalid carriage, the Invacar being the only 1957-announced (and indeed, the last) new, invalid three-wheeler to do so.

In April 1958, the Ministry instructed the Invacar company to increase the size of the Mk 10's front wheel from ten to twelve inches. This increase, and other alterations to its appearance, resulted in the Invacar Mk 10A. Production ended in April 1959 with none of the 1003 examples produced known to exist at the time of writing.

Shown is a 1957 artist's impression of an Invacar Mk 10, which was used in a contemporary advertisement for Schroder tire valves.

THE A.C. ACEDES

It has often been stated that the 1957 A.C. Acedes was based on the
A.C. Petite minicar of 1953. Although there was a slight passing
resemblance in the all-aluminum body, the two machines were
actually entirely unrelated, the Acedes having a completely different
chassis and power unit, and the latter being the Ministry standardized
Villiers Mk 9E engine.

In September 1958, a 72-volt electric version of the Acedes
was introduced, primarily for Ministry of Health issue, while the

petrol variant received many detail alterations over the years. Those alterations included glass windows from 1961, the Villiers Mk 11E engine from 1962, and a sliding seat from 1966.

Although technically replaced by the fiberglass bodied Acedes Mk 14 of 1967, the original metal-bodied Acedes underwent very limited production in both petrol and electric forms and in hard and soft-top forms until 1972, with 13,155 petrol and 2,182 electric machines being produced in total.

Shown is a 1966 AC Acedes Mk 12.

THE
BARRETT
MINOR &
MIDGET

The Bristol-based company of W&F Barrett Ltd. had built open invalid tricycles in the 1940's but in the 1950s and 1960s, it was contracted to build two "special-case" vehicles for the Ministry of Health. The first, introduced in 1956, was the Barrett Minor, a very small vehicle at 8 ft. long and 32 ft., 2 in. wide. It was issued to "small persons with short arm reach."

In 1959, the Minor was replaced by the only slightly larger Barrett Midget, developed for "persons up to 4 ft. 6 in. tall." As with the Minor, a rear-mounted 197cc Villiers Mk 9E provided the power. A new design of fiberglass body, finished in green, was fitted for the Midget.

With all production purchased by the Ministry of Health, the W & F Barrett Ltd. supply contracts were canceled in 1968, following the formation of the Department of Health and Social Security, which decided that most users of Barrett machines could be catered to just as well by the Tippen Delta.

Three Barrett Midgets but no Barrett Minors are known to survive.

Shown is the only known surviving publicity picture for the Barrett Minor.

THE TIPPEN DELTA

Introduced in 1955, the Coventry-built Tippen Delta was one of the earliest "full-bodied" invalid three-wheelers and an early exponent of fiberglass construction. It was also the first invalid three-wheeler to incorporate a sliding door.

Throughout its long production life, there were several variants of the petrol Delta, the original having a Villiers Mk 8E engine, wire wheels, a single headlight, and a dark blue finish. The Delta 2 of 1958 had a Villiers Mk 9E unit and was finished in a paler blue color.

The 1959 Delta 3 had twin headlights. The 1966 Delta 6 had 12-inch wheels, whilst the 1968 Delta 8 again underwent a face-lift and gained a much squarer frontal profile.

In 1965, a 36-volt electrically-propelled version of the Tippen Delta, using the same body as the petrol Deltas 6, 7, & 8, was introduced specifically for the Ministry of Health. Production of the petrol Delta ended in 1970, whilst the electric version continued until 1976.

Shown is the youngest known surviving Tippen Delta, the 1974 example of the Momence Motor Museum, Illinois.

THE INVACAR MK 12

Introduced in 1960, the Invacar Mk 12 had a fiberglass body, while early examples had a two-tone color scheme of peacock blue with a white roof. The scheme was changed in 1967 to all over pale blue. The power source was initially the Villiers Mk 9E engine, but this was replaced in April 1962 by the broadly similar Villiers Mk 11E unit.

In production for eleven years, this particular Invacar had six variants. The original Mk 12 gave way to the Mk 12A in April 1962 with the incorporation of glass side windows and the Villiers Mk 11E engine. The 12B of April 1966 had a sliding seat. The 12C of April 1967 had a hydraulic front brake. The 12D of April 1968 had larger headlights, while the 12E of April 1969 was fitted with the new "parallelogram" front suspension of the A.C. Acedes Mk 14.

The Invacar Mk 12 was to be the last "true" Invacar. Its 1971 replacement, the Model 70, was wholly an A.C. Acedes design.

Shown is a 1963 Mk 12A owned by the Museum of disABILITY History.

THE A.C. ACEDES
MK 14 & 15

By the mid 1960s, the A.C. Acedes of 1957 was starting to look a little old-fashioned, and so, in April 1967, A.C. Cars Ltd. introduced the new A.C. Acedes Mk 14. Mechanically identical to the old model, in that it was powered by the Villiers Mk 11E engine, the new Mk 14 had a fully fiberglass body.

The Acedes Mk 14 also saw the introduction of the "Drop-Open" sliding door, in which the door was opened from the outside by turning the recessed handle downwards and then pulling the

door outwards from the vehicle. The door then tilted by pivoting on its bottom edge, actually falling outwards entirely unchecked for a distance of about eight inches. It was then slid forward to give access to the interior.

Available only in petrol form, detail modifications to the rear suspension after a short time in production resulted in the Acedes Mk 15. Production of the fiberglass Acedes ceased in 1971, with 5,928 models were produced in total.

Shown is a 1967 publicity picture for the AC Acedes Mk 14.

THE
MODEL 70

The invalid three-wheeler reached its zenith in June 1971 with the introduction of the Model 70, which replaced both the fiberglass A.C. Acedes and the Invacar Mk 12. Although produced jointly by both A.C. Cars Ltd. and Invacar Ltd., the Model 70 was entirely an A.C. design from the ground up.

Hailed by users as a great improvement over previous invalid three-wheelers, the Model 70 was much faster and easier to drive due to its 493cc Steyr-Puch flat-twin engine and Salisbury variable belt transmission, which eliminated the manual gearbox of the Villiers-powered tricycles. Tailored to suit a wide range of disabilities, the Model 70 could be ordered with either a tiller bar, handlebar, or wheel steering.

During July 1976, the Department of Health and Social Security announced the closure of the Invalid Vehicle Service in favor of the recently introduced Mobility Allowance. Production of the Model 70 ended in March 1978.

Shown is a 1976 Invacar Model 70.

MINISTRY
OF HEALTH
MODEL
NUMBERING

When the National Health Service began to purchase invalid three-wheelers in large numbers from 1948 onwards, the Ministry of Health introduced its own internal model numbering system to identify each general type of vehicle ordered. Listed are all such numbers allocated to powered machines:

M.o.H. Model 39 .... Various early petrol vehicles
M.o.H. Model 39A .... Tippen Convalite, 70cc
M.o.H. Model 39B .... Tippen Convalite, 150cc
M.o.H. Model 41 .... Barrett M25
M.o.H. Model 42 .... Invacar Westcliff (Mk 6)
M.o.H. Model 42A .... Invacar Mk 8
M.o.H. Model 43 .... A.C. All-Weather Tricycle
M.o.H. Model 44 .... Argson Electric
M.o.H. Model 49 .... Tippen Delta Mk 1
M.o.H. Model 52 .... Invacar Mk 8A
M.o.H. Model 53 .... Vernon Invalid Car Mk 1 & 2
M.o.H. Model 53A .... Vernon Invalid Car Mk 3
M.o.H. Model 54 .... Harper Mk 1 (electric)
M.o.H. Model 55 .... Harper Mk 1 (petrol)
M.o.H. Model 54A .... Harper Mk 6 (electric)
M.o.H. Model 55A .... Harper Mk 6 (petrol)
M.o.H. Model 56 .... Invacar Mk 10 & 10A
M.o.H. Model 57 .... A.C. Acedes Mk 1 - 12
M.o.H. Model 58 .... Barrett Minor
M.o.H. Model 59 .... Tippen Delta Mk 2 - 8
M.o.H. Model 60 .... Barrett Midget
M.o.H. Model 62 .... Invacar Mk 11
M.o.H. Model 64 .... A.C. Acedes Electric
M.o.H. Model 65 .... Stanley Mk 7
M.o.H. Model 66 .... Invacar Mk 12 - 12E
DHSS Model 67 .... A.C. Acedes Mk 14 & 15
DHSS Model 69E .... Tippen Delta Electric
DHSS Model 70 .... A.C./Invacar Model 70

DEFINITIONS

1. **Bath Chair** – chair on wheels intended for use by women and the invalid. It was devised by James Heath, of Bath England about 1750. For the next three-quarters of a century it rivaled the sedan chair and ultimately superseded it as a form of conveyance in Great Britain. The most common variety was supported on two wheels joined by an axle beneath the seat, with a small pivoting wheel in front supporting the footrest.

   The chair could be pushed from behind and steered by a long curved rod connected to the front wheel and controlled by the occupant. The whole conveyance was designed on flowing lines. The bath chair was especially popular during Victorian times, when it was used at seaside resorts.

2. **DVLA** – Driver and Vehicle Licensing Agency

3. **V 765 Application** – form to register a vehicle in England under its original number. Useful to register old vehicles.

4. **SIBA Dynastart** – an early starter and battery charger

5. **Microcars:** In the UK, the general definition of "microcars" includes economy vehicles with either three or four wheels powered by petrol engines of not usually more than 700cc (in the United States, the upper limit is usually 1,000cc) or battery electric propulsion, and generally manufactured since 1945, but these parameters can be varied if justified by vehicle interest.

PHOTO
CREDITS

CPSIA information can be obtained
at www.ICGtesting.com
Printed in the USA
BVHW011206211020
591502BV00006BA/461

9 780984 598380